Overflow of the Heart

Esther Valimont

BookLeaf Publishing

India | USA | UK

Presentation by *BookLeaf Publishing*

Web: www.bookleafpub.com

E-mail: info@bookleafpub.com

ISBN: 9789357446785

First edition 2022

DEDICATION

To My Family (That means all of you;)

Who have always encouraged me to chase after God and His call.

You inspire me with your faith and obedience to the Lord and I'm so thankful that He has given us each other.

I hope that through this I can share a taste of who He has proven Himself to be in my life, and scratch the surface of who I know He is, and wants to be in yours.

All Glory to God!

ACKNOWLEDGEMENT

Most of the inspiration for the poems in this book have come from scripture, as well as my personal experiences.

PREFACE

This is my first attempt at poetry so please forgive me if my words cannot convey the depth of the message I so desire to share.

I have written this in an attempt to show a small portion of the glory of the God who has never left me.

Growing up I used to read about David spending time with the Lord while watching his father's sheep.

While I don't have any skill on the harp or with a sling, I did enjoy sitting with my very small flock of sheep and talking to God, and learning to know Him as my best friend.

He is always ready to listen and advise and I will never be able to find the words to thank Him enough.

I hope you enjoy the musings of one who will always be amazed to be called a friend of God.

Mine

You are mine.
Can you ever question my love?
What more could I do to show you the depths of
my love for you?
Why do you doubt?
Oh raise a shout for the bridegroom approaches!
I come on the wind, your heart to win.
Our time at arm's length draws to a close.
Oh to experience the intertwining of our souls.
To hold you and never let go!
For you are mine and our love is divine.

Who is like the Lord?

Who is like the Lord?
Who else should be adored?
He makes the heavens ring,
and makes my heart sing.
Who is like the Lord?
All honor is due His name,
creation sings His praise.
Who is like the Lord?
He who clothes the flowers,
clothes me in His power.
Who is like the Lord?
The one who paints the sky,
wipes every tear from my eye.
Who is like the Lord?
He sees the heart of man,
He alone is the great I Am.

What is Enough?

Where do you turn when your dreams come true
and you still feel empty?
When the job doesn't satisfy and family doesn't
fill the hole.
Why isn't it enough?
What am I missing?
There is only one who can fill the hole inside.
Only one who can truly satisfy.
Why?
Because He made you.
He knows you.
Only when He is in all things will they satisfy
you.

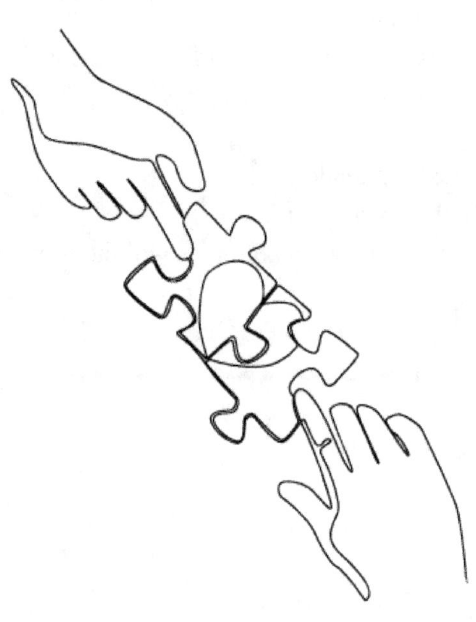

Great is the Lord

Great is the Lord, and worthy to be praised.
Great is the Lord, the author of our days.
He paints the skies with fire at dawn.
From heavenly places He fills my heart with
song.
He waters the earth with dew and rain.
He comforts me in my sorrow and works all
things for my gain.
The one who is Holy loved me when I was
profane.
Then with His pain, bought my freedom and
gave me a new name.
He became my claim to fame;
Oh Great is the Lord and worthy to be praised!

What is Love?

We like the picture of love that's all roses and
butterflies, but is that all there is?
Wouldn't we become bored with a life constantly
skipping through meadows, watching rain from
behind closed windows?
Love is strong, it overlooks wrongs.
Love is choosing to forgive as long as you live.
Love is fighting to save someone when they turn
and spit in your face.
Love is willing to be despised for the chance at
saving a life.
Love is choosing to lose someone to save them.
Love is never starting something you know you
won't finish.
Love is freeing someone who will never thank
you for your sacrifice.
Love is free will and waiting.
Love is tears without fear.
Love is pain for another's gain.
Love is God's nature because,
God is Love.

Praise

Oh Lord, let my praise be sweet to you!
Let the intentions of my heart be pleasing to
you.
Anoint my lips to speak truth to the nations.
Teach my hands to bring healing to the broken.
Show me how to battle for peace;
and keep my soul at ease.

Who is Good?

We ask how a good God can allow evil but we
ask out of our scope.
Can you with a breath give life?
Are worlds formed at your words?
Did you raise the mountains and give borders to
the seas?
Do galaxies form from your imaginings?
Do you knit together each new life before it's
even seen?
How can we hope to understand the thoughts of
one so high?
How can we scoff when we receive the desire of
His absence in our lives?

Who is Like Our God?

Who is like our God?
He makes the earth to tremble and also sees the
sparrow.
Darkness flees from the one who knows me.
The rivers and seas obey
the one who knows my name.
Oh exalt Him among the nations.
Make Him famous!
For He is good and true and He loves you!

Who are We?

How can you not love someone who died to save
you before he knew you?
How can you despise someone who loved you
when you hated Him?
How can you accuse Him of not caring when He
gave up everything?
How can you question someone who is so far
above you?
How can you assume the moral high ground to
someone so grand?
How do you assume to know God?
How do you question His love?
How do you not love Him in return?

Honor where it's Due

Give the Lord the Honor due to His name.
Praise to the one who overcame the grave.
He makes the earth and mountains tremble.
Exalt Him in His holy temple.
Oh give the Lord the honor due to His name.

Praise in Pain

Where do you turn when the sorrow is too great?
When you've bruised your knees in prayer and
the answer isn't there?
What peace is left to find when you beg for
healing and find death instead?
What is the correct response?
They say the sweetest praise is born from the
place of your deepest pain.
If this is true then there can be nothing so sweet
as ours.
For in this moment when none can understand
your ways,
we choose to give our praise to the one who
understands our pain.

A Song of Thanks

I thank you oh Lord for your goodness to me.
You are always so faithful to me.
I will praise you with my life, soul, and heart.
You will always be the constant in my life.
When confusion, fear, and uncertainty strike,
I will follow you into the light.
You love me when I am unlovable.
You understand and guide me when I don't even
know myself.
You love when others judge, and faithfully lead
me back to truth.
When darkness and death try to overpower me,
you, only you surround me.
You will never leave, never deceive.
You will never use, never abuse.
Your love is the love to weigh all others against.
Your love is the love I must give.
You teach that by dying to self we can truly live.
Teach me to praise you with my life, and not
only with my lips.

Who does God say we are?

We were once perfect, now fallen.
Enslaved then redeemed, those condemned set
free.
The Lord created a perfect people,
Grieved as they turned from Him,
Choosing rather to be slaves to sin.
The spurned creator gave Himself to redeem
them.
Then again gave them free choice to love Him or
leave Him.
Who does He say that we are?
Loved, chosen, redeemed, and free
to choose to remain who He says we can be,
or run back to our slavery to lesser things.

Who is like Yahweh?

Who is like Yahweh?
Who can know His ways?
He makes the seas to roar,
He rides above the waves.
His glory is unknowable,
His mercy is unsearchable.
He alone gives wisdom and might,
In Him alone will my soul delight.
He knows the hearts of Man,
and still He delights in them.
Great is Yahweh and Worthy to be Praised!

Confounding the Wise

Oh how wise we become in our own eyes!

We reach for the skies to obtain a prize that we think applies but to our surprise when we look past the lies we see the disguise, hear the cries "Loose us from these ties that bind, and save us from our demise!" We analyze, revise and find no matter how much we improvise or chastise, we cannot devise a way to rise above our demise until...

a compromise.

We call to God who hears our cries, sees our demise and does not despise but rather calls Himself our ally.

He inserts Himself into the mix of our doomed lives, applies our debt to His account and with His own death buys our freedom as His prize.
Then diving into the divide between life and death, He defeats the grave and invites us with Him to rise.
To die to self, turn from our sin and despise our disguise made of lies and instead to cry "I'll press toward the prize that His blood buys!" and

follow Him to new heights, where there are no more goodbyes.

Forever to walk by His side, not a tear in our eyes because now we're with the one who has come for His bride.

Our Maker, then Savior, now Husband, HE IS ADONI.

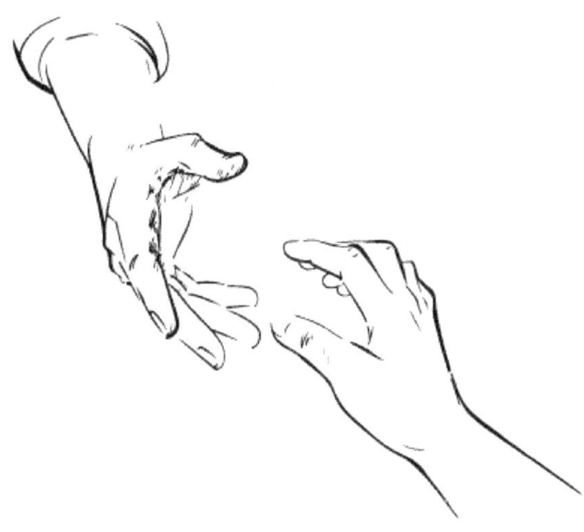

What can I give to the King

What can I give to the King
who made everything?
What could my life bring
as an offering?
What do I give to the one
who gave me His only Son?
What can I impart
to the one who made my heart?
What can I give to the King
who made everything?
How can I show my love
to the one who gave me His Son?
What is an offering
that my life can bring?
I'll give my everything
all to the King.

A Friend of God

Oh how sweet is it for your lover to be your creator?
For your everything to be wrapped up in the one that made, then gave you everything.
Who could be better?
Where not a secret can exist and no back will ever be turned.
Never to wonder what the other feels for, and about you.
No fear in coming and being, "a bother".
Never to cry alone and wonder, "Do they know my pain? Will they ever understand? Would they even care?".
Never to be thrown aside for another.
Never to become boring, old or used up.
Never to be left behind at the end.
Always to be loved, cherished, understood, and desired.
To be available at any moment and never apart.
Oh how sweet for your maker to be more than a friend!

I will Boast in the Lord

Do I consider myself a great scholar or poet?
Do I boast in my own eloquence?
I do not; but I do boast in my King.
I obey when He speaks and He makes my words
as honey and oil.
He alone gives wisdom and beauty.